Get Motoring!

Cars

by Dalton Rains

FOCUS READERS

SCOUT

www.focusreaders.com

Focus Readers is distributed by North Star Editions:
sales@northstareditions.com | 888-417-0195

Produced for Focus Readers by Red Line Editorial.

Photographs ©: Shutterstock Images, cover, 1, 4, 7 (top), 7 (bottom), 9 (top), 9 (bottom), 11 (top), 11 (bottom), 13 (top), 13 (bottom), 15 (top), 15 (bottom), 16 (top left), 16 (top right); iStockphoto, 16 (bottom left), 16 (bottom right)

Library of Congress Cataloging-in-Publication Data
Names: Rains, Dalton, author.
Title: Cars / by Dalton Rains.
Description: Mendota Heights, MN : Focus Readers, [2024] | Series: Get motoring! | Includes index. | Audience: Grades K-1 |
Identifiers: LCCN 2023031712 (print) | LCCN 2023031713 (ebook) | ISBN 9798889980087 (hardcover) | ISBN 9798889980513 (paperback) | ISBN 9798889981367 (pdf) | ISBN 9798889980940 (ebook)
Subjects: LCSH: Automobiles--Juvenile literature.
Classification: LCC TL147 .R363 2024 (print) | LCC TL147 (ebook) | DDC 629.222--dc23/eng/20230728
LC record available at https://lccn.loc.gov/2023031712
LC ebook record available at https://lccn.loc.gov/2023031713

Printed in the United States of America
Mankato, MN
012024

About the Author

Dalton Rains is a writer and editor who lives in Minnesota.

Table of Contents

road

Cars

Cars drive on roads. Cars help people go from place to place.

Some cars are for driving fast. Other cars are used to drive families.

Parts

A car uses an **engine** or a **motor** to move. Some cars use gasoline. Others use electricity.

A car has doors on the sides.
It has a **trunk** in the back.
Inside a car, there is one
seat for the driver.
There are also seats
for **passengers**.

seat

passengers

Uses

Many people use cars every day. They might drive to work or school. They might drive to stores, too.

Some people use cars
to drive others.
These cars are called taxis.

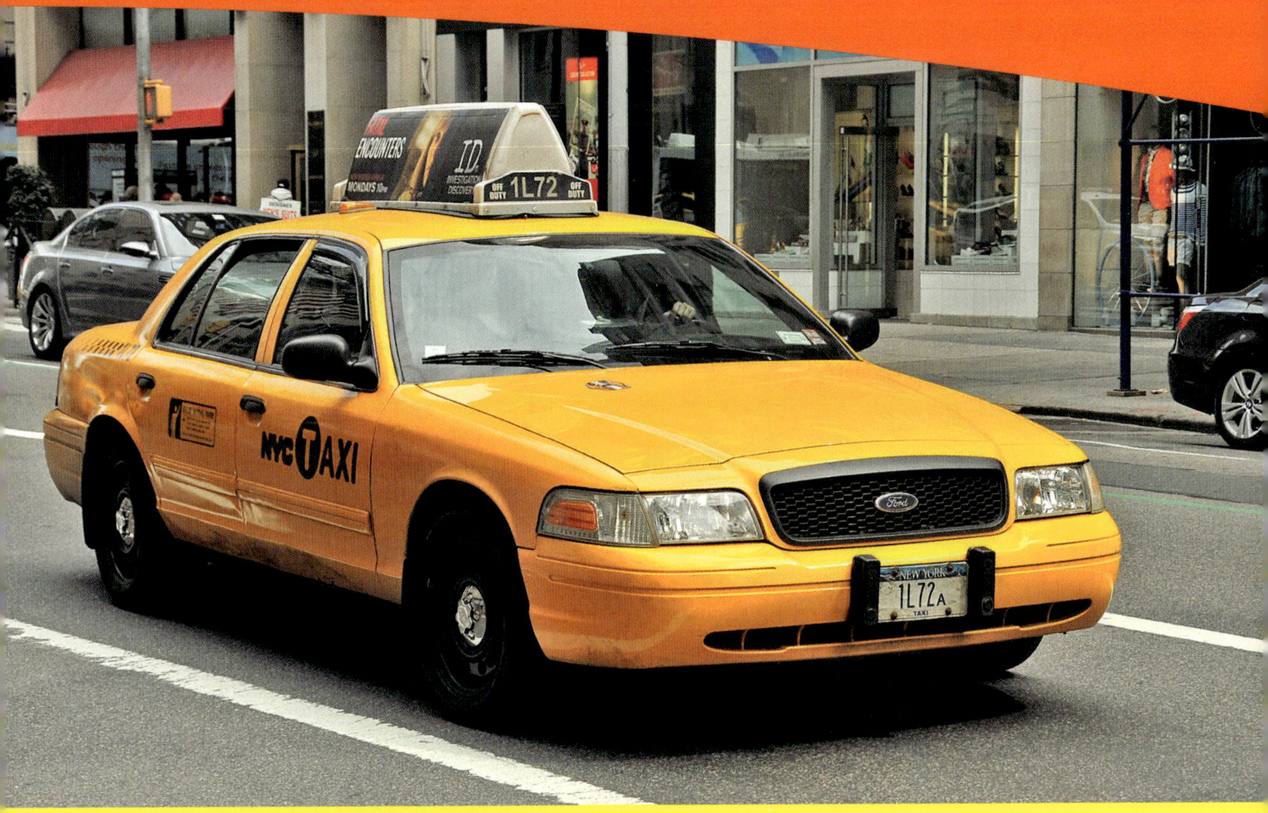
OFF DUTY 1L72 OFF DUTY
NYC TAXI
NEW YORK
1L72A
TAXI

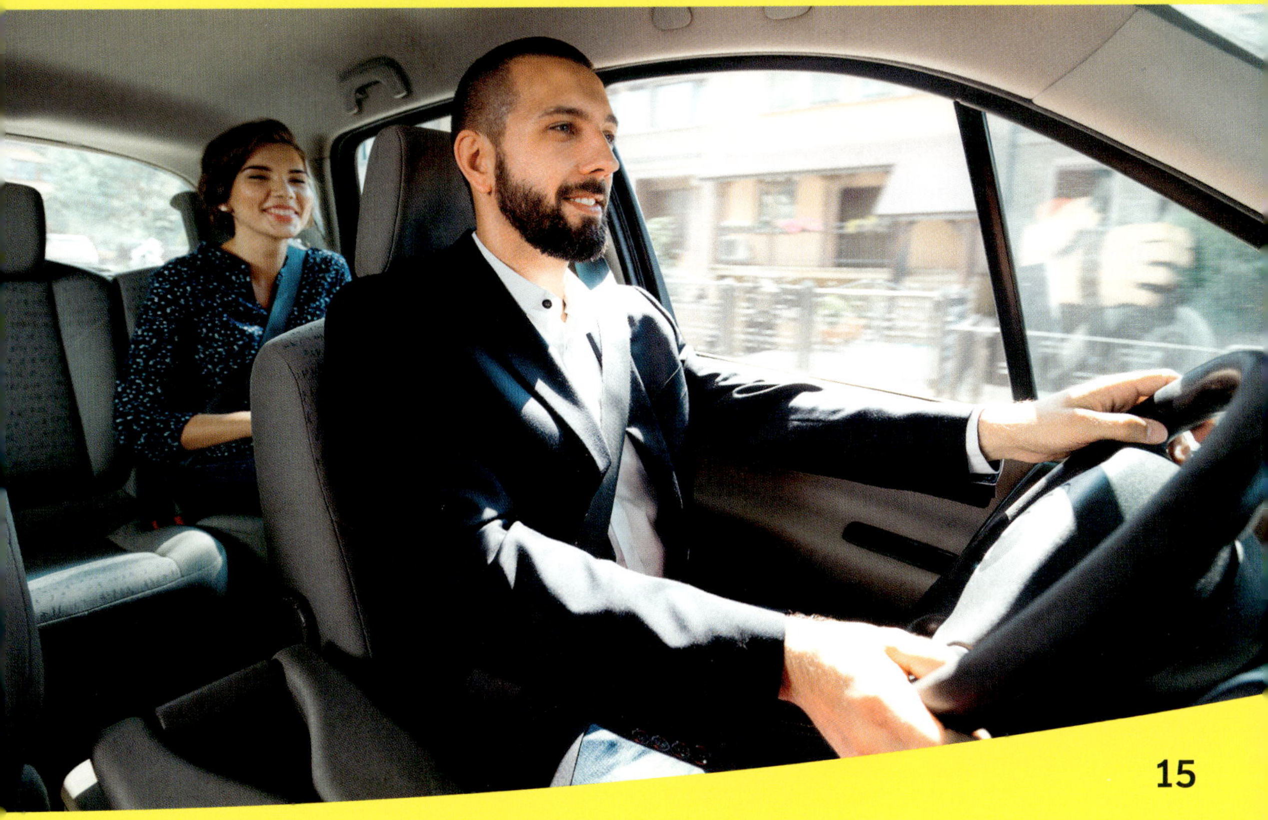

Glossary

engine

passengers

motor

trunk

Index